I Know That!

Seeing

Claire Llewellyn

FRANKLIN WATTS
LONDON • SYDNEY

First published in 2004 by Franklin Watts
96 Leonard Street, London EC2A 4XD

Franklin Watts Australia
45-51 Huntley Street, Alexandria, NSW 2015

Text copyright © Claire Llewellyn 2004
Design and concept © Franklin Watts 2004

Series advisers: Gill Matthews, non-fiction literacy
*   consultant and Inset trainer*
Editor: Rachel Cooke
Series design: Peter Scoulding
Designer: James Marks
Photography: Ray Moller unless otherwise credited
Acknowledgements: Harold Chapman/Topham: 11t.
Corbis: 10. Chris Fairclough/Franklin Watts: 16, 18, 21r.
Michael Gore/Ecoscene: 9tr.Klein/Still Pictures: 13tr.
Mostyn/Eye Ubiquitous: 9b, 15t. Paul Seheult/Eye Ubiquitous: 19.
Joseph Sohm/Image Works/Topham: 14. Thanks to our models, including Vanessa Dang, Sophie
Hall, Latifah Harris, Thomas Howe, Amelia Menicou, Spencer Mulchay and Ishar Sehgal.

A CIP catalogue record for this book is available from the British Library.

ISBN: 0 7496 5723 5

Printed in Malaysia

Contents

We see with our eyes

Every day we use our eyes to see the world around us. Seeing is one of our senses.

▶ *We use our eyes to read a book…*

4

choose some fruit...

We have five senses. They are seeing, hearing, tasting, smelling and touching.

pour a drink...

and look in the mirror.

5

Looking at eyes

We have two eyes on our face.

▼ *Our eyes can be brown...*

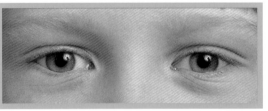

blue...

grey...

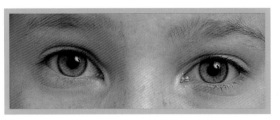

or green.

Eyes have many different parts.

Find a mirror and look at your eyes. What colour are they?

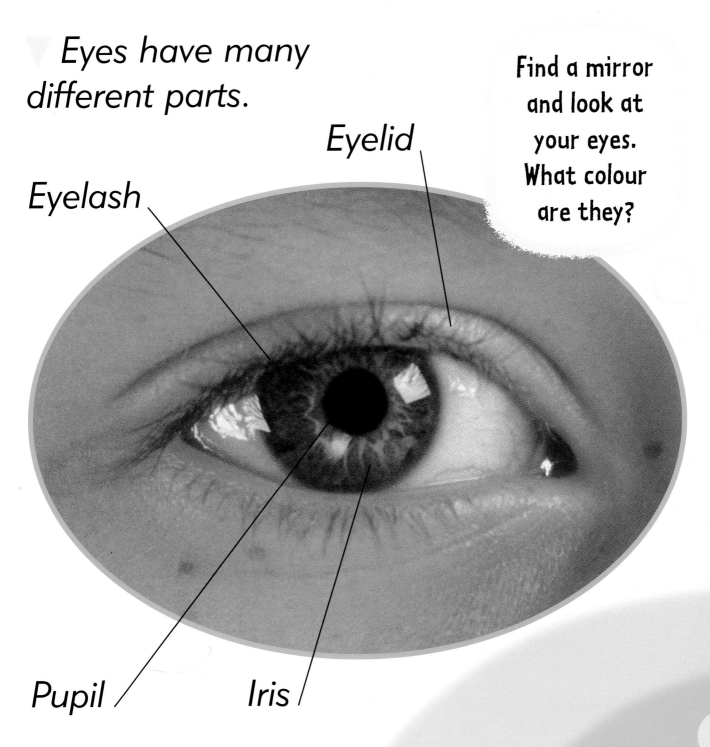

Eyelash

Eyelid

Pupil

Iris

7

We need light to see

We see when light enters our eyes. When there is no light, we cannot see.

When we switch the light off at night, it is too dark to see.

A torch gives us light to see in the dark.

An owl feeds at night. Its big eyes help it to see in the dark.

We see in colour

Our eyes can see the colours in the world around us.

We see all the colours of the rainbow.

10

We stop when we see a red light; we go when the light turns green.

Bees see in colour, too. When they see colourful flowers, they land on them and feed.

We like colourful clothes.

Using our eyes

We use our eyes to see whether things are big or small.

We can see the jumper is too big!

12

We use our eyes to see what is near or far away.

A cat's eyes tell it how far it has to jump to land safely.

We can see the toy is nearer than the chair.

Keeping safe

Our eyes help us find our way.
They keep us safe.

We can follow the signs.

We look both ways before we cross the road.

How do your eyes help to keep you safe on your way to school?

We see *if something* is in our way.

15

Wearing glasses

Some people cannot see clearly. They have glasses to help them.

This girl is having her eyes tested.

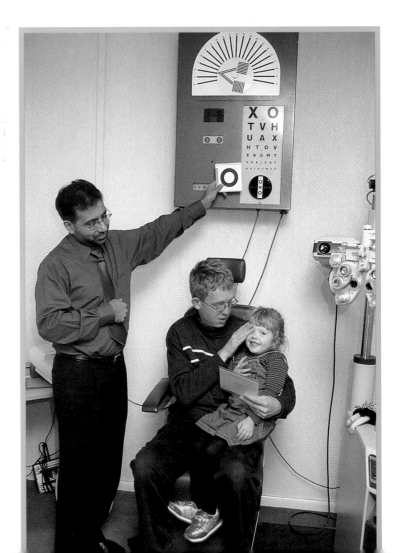

Glasses help people to see clearly.

We go to the optician's to have our eyes tested. Opticians are eye experts.

Some people wear contact lenses instead.

Some people cannot see

Blind people see very badly.
Some blind people cannot
see anything
at all.

Some blind
people have a
guide dog to
help them find
their way.

Blind people read letters made of dots.

When blind people read, which of their five senses are they using?

Looking after our eyes

Our eyes are very important.
We must look after them.

▶ *Always read with plenty of light...*

and wear sunglasses on a sunny day.

Don't look at the Sun. It can damage your eyes.

When we blink, our eyelids wipe our eyes. This keeps them clean.

Have you had an eye test? Every child should have one.

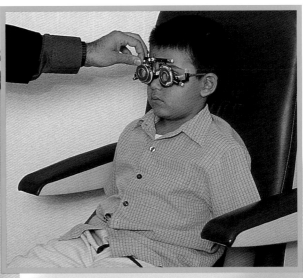

I know that...

1 We use our eyes to see.

2 Seeing is one of our senses.

3 Our eyes can be brown, blue, grey or green.

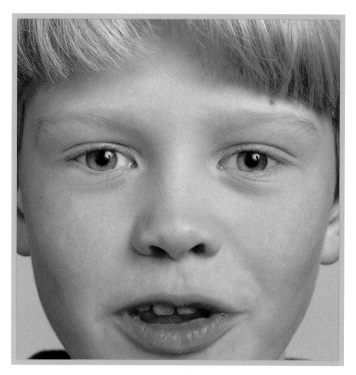

4 We need light to see.

5 Our eyes see colours.

6 Our eyes tell us if something is big, small, near or far.

7 Seeing helps to keep us safe.

8 Glasses help people to see more clearly.

9 Blind people see very badly or not at all.

10 We must look after our eyes.

Index

About this book

I Know That! is designed to introduce children to the process of gathering information and using reference books, one of the key skills needed to begin more formal learning at school. For this reason, each book's structure reflects the information books children will use later in their learning career – with key information in the main text and additional facts and ideas in the captions. The panels give an opportunity for further activities, ideas or discussions. The contents page and index are helpful reference guides.

The language is carefully chosen to be accessible to children just beginning to read. Illustrations support the text but also give information in their own right; active consideration and discussion of images is another key referencing skill. The main aim of the series is to build confidence – showing children how much they already know and giving them the ability to gather new information for themselves. With this in mind, the *I know that...* section at the end of the book is a simple way for children to revisit what they already know as well as what they have learnt from reading the book.